"IT'S A CHRISTMAS MIRACLE!"

CHRISTMAS 2006

MERRY CHRISTMAS, COMP.

—DAN7 AttO7

¡OIGA!

Sleigh Bells Ring

LINDA NELSON STOCKS

Andrews McMeel
Publishing, LLC
Kansas City

06 07 08 09 10 WKT 10 9 8 7 6 5 4 3 2 1

ISBN-13: 978-0-7407-6073-0
ISBN-10: 0-7407-6073-4

Library of Congress Control Number: 2006923249

Book design by Holly Camerlinck

www.andrewsmcmeel.com

ATTENTION: SCHOOLS AND BUSINESSES

Andrews McMeel books are available at quantity discounts with bulk purchase for educational, business, or sales promotional use. For information, please write to: Special Sales Department, Andrews McMeel Publishing, LLC, 4520 Main Street, Kansas City, Missouri 64111.

Until one feels the spirit of Christmas, there is no Christmas.

All else is outward display ~ so much tinsel and decorations.

For it isn't the holly, it isn't the snow.

It isn't the tree nor the firelight's glow.

It's the warmth that comes to the hearts of men when the Christmas spirit returns again.

ANONYMOUS

Christmas is the gentlest,
loveliest festival of the
revolving year—and yet,
for all that, when it speaks,
its voice has strong authority.

W. J. CAMERON

H e who has not

Christmas

in his heart

will never find it

under a tree.

✤ ROY L. SMITH

The joy of brightening other lives,

bearing each other's burdens,

easing others' loads,

and supplanting empty hearts and lives

with generous gifts becomes for us

the magic of Christmas.

W. C. Jones

*P*erhaps the best
Yuletide decoration
is being wreathed

in smiles.

❧ ANONYMOUS

© Linda Nelson Stocks

$\mathcal{W}$hile $\mathcal{I}$ relish
our warm months,
winter forms our character
and brings out our best.

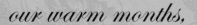 THOMAS H. ALLEN

For centuries men have kept an appointment with Christmas.

Christmas means fellowship, feasting, giving and receiving, a time of good cheer, home.

W. J. RONALD TUCKER

The happiness and love on

this one day

Bring thoughts which warm

and cheer.

May we keep Christmas in

our hearts

Through every day of all the year.

GERTRUDE B. HOLMAN,
"THE LITTLE THINGS AT CHRISTMAS"

*Christmas waves
a magic wand over this world,
and behold, everything is
softer and more beautiful.*

🎕 NORMAN VINCENT PEALE

$\mathcal{L}$ike snowflakes,

my Christmas memories

gather and dance~

each beautiful, unique,

and too soon gone.

❧ DEBORAH WHIPP

This is the message
of Christmas:

We are never alone.

❧ TAYLOR CALDWELL

Christmas!

The very word brings joy to our hearts.

No matter how we may dread the rush,

the long Christmas lists for gifts and cards

to be bought and given ~

when Christmas Day comes

there is still the same warm feeling we had

as children, the same warmth

that enfolds our hearts and our homes.

JOAN WINMILL BROWN

*At Christmas play
and make good cheer,
For Christmas comes
but once a year*

❦ THOMAS TUSSER, "THE FARMER'S DAILY DIET"

©Linda L Nelson

At Christmas,

all roads lead home.

Marjorie Holmes

Winter is the time of promise because there is so little to do—or because you can now and then permit yourself the luxury of thinking so.

❦ STANLEY CRAWFORD

*Christmas is sights,
especially the sights of Christmas
reflected in the eyes of a child.*

SUGAR
PLUM
TOY
SHOPPE

❧ WILLIAM SAROYAN

Yes, Virginia, there is a Santa Claus. He exists as certainly as love and generosity and devotion exist, and you know that they abound and give to your life its highest beauty and joy. Alas! how dreary would be the world if there were no Santa Claus!

FROM AN EDITORIAL WRITTEN BY FRANCIS P. CHURCH
FOR THE *NEW YORK SUN*, SEPTEMBER 21, 1897

They err who think Santa Claus comes down through the chimney; he really enters through the heart.

 Mrs. Paul M. Ell

Christmas is the season for kindling the fire of hospitality in the hall, the genial flame of charity in the heart.

WASHINGTON IRVING

What is Christmas?

It is tenderness for the past, courage

for the present, hope for the future.

It is a fervent wish that every cup

may overflow with blessings rich

and eternal, and that every path

may lead to peace.

AGNES M. PHARO

Christmas Eve was a night of song
that wrapped itself about you like a shawl.

But it warmed more than your body.

It warmed your heart . . . filled it, too,

with melody that would last forever.

BESS STREETER ALDRICH, *SONG OF YEARS*

*E*very time we love,

every time we give,

it's Christmas.

❧ DALE EVANS

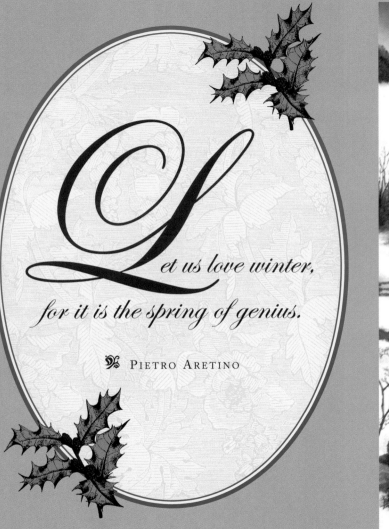

$\mathscr{L}$et us love winter,

for it is the spring of genius.

❧ PIETRO ARETINO

Sing hey! Sing hey!

For Christmas Day;

Twine mistletoe and holly.

For a friendship glows

In winter snows,

And so let's all be jolly!

ANONYMOUS

There is a privacy about it which no other season gives you. . . . In spring, summer, and fall people sort of have an open season on each other; only in the winter, in the country, can you have longer, quiet stretches when you can savor belonging to yourself.

— RUTH STOUT

Gifts of time and love

are surely the basic ingredients

of a truly merry Christmas.

PEG BRACKEN

Our hearts grow tender

with childhood memories and

love of kindred, and we are better

throughout the year for having,

in spirit, become a child again

at Christmas-time.

❧ LAURA INGALLS WILDER

In seed time learn,

in harvest teach,

in winter enjoy.

WILLIAM BLAKE

The best of all gifts around

any Christmas tree:

the presence of a happy family

all wrapped up in each other.

BURTON HILLIS

©Linda L Nelson

©Linda Nelson

Christmas is most truly

Christmas

when we celebrate it

by giving the light of love

to those who need it most.

RUTH CARTER STAPLETON

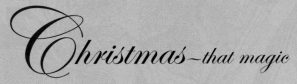 *Christmas*—that magic
blanket that wraps itself about us, that something so
intangible that it is like a fragrance. It may
weave a spell of nostalgia. Christmas may be a
day of feasting, or of prayer, but always it will be
a day of remembrance—a day in which we think
of everything we have ever loved.

Augusta E. Rundel

Winter, a lingering season,

is a time to gather golden moments,

embark upon a sentimental journey,

and enjoy every idle hour.

❧ JOHN BOSWELL

Whatever else be lost among the years,
    Let us keep Christmas still a shining thing:
Whatever doubts assail us, or what fears,
    Let us hold close one day, remembering
Its poignant meaning for the hearts of men.
    Let us get back our childlike faith again.

GRACE NOLL CROWELL

Winter is the time for comfort,
for good food and warmth,
for the touch of a friendly hand,
and for a talk beside the fire:
It is the time for home.

❧ DAME EDITH SITWELL

*C*hristmas, in its final essence,
is for grown people who have forgotten

what children know.

Christmas is for whoever is old enough

to have denied the unquenchable

spirit of man.

❦ MARGARET COUSINS

©Linda Nelson Stocks

Peace on earth
will come to stay,
When we live
Christmas
every day.

HELEN STEINER RICE

Christmas...

is not an eternal event at all,

but a piece of one's home

that one carries in one's heart.

❦ FREYA STARK